Lonely planet Kids

INFOGRAPHIC

GUIDE TO THE GLOBE

WRITTEN BY
ELIZA BERKOWITZ

ILLUSTRATED BY
GWEN KERAVAL

ACKNOWLEDGMENTS

Publishing Director: Piers Pickard
Publisher: Hanna Otero
Editor: Nicole Otto
Art Director: Ryan Thomann
Designers: Ryan Thomann and Gwen Keraval
Print Production: Lisa Ford
Author: Eliza Berkowitz
Illustrator: Gwen Keraval
Thanks to: Tina García, Kate Baker, Joe Fullman

Published in November 2020 by Lonely Planet Global Ltd
CRN: 554153
ISBN: 978-1-83869-226-1
www.lonelyplanetkids.com
© Lonely Planet 2020

Printed in China
10 9 8 7 6 5 4 3 2 1

STAY IN TOUCH
lonelyplanet.com/contact

Lonely Planet Offices

Ireland
Digital Depot, Roe Lane (off Thomas St), Digital Hub, Dublin 8, D08 TCV4

USA
230 Franklin Road, Building 2B, Franklin, TN 37064
T: 615-988-9713

TABLE OF CONTENTS

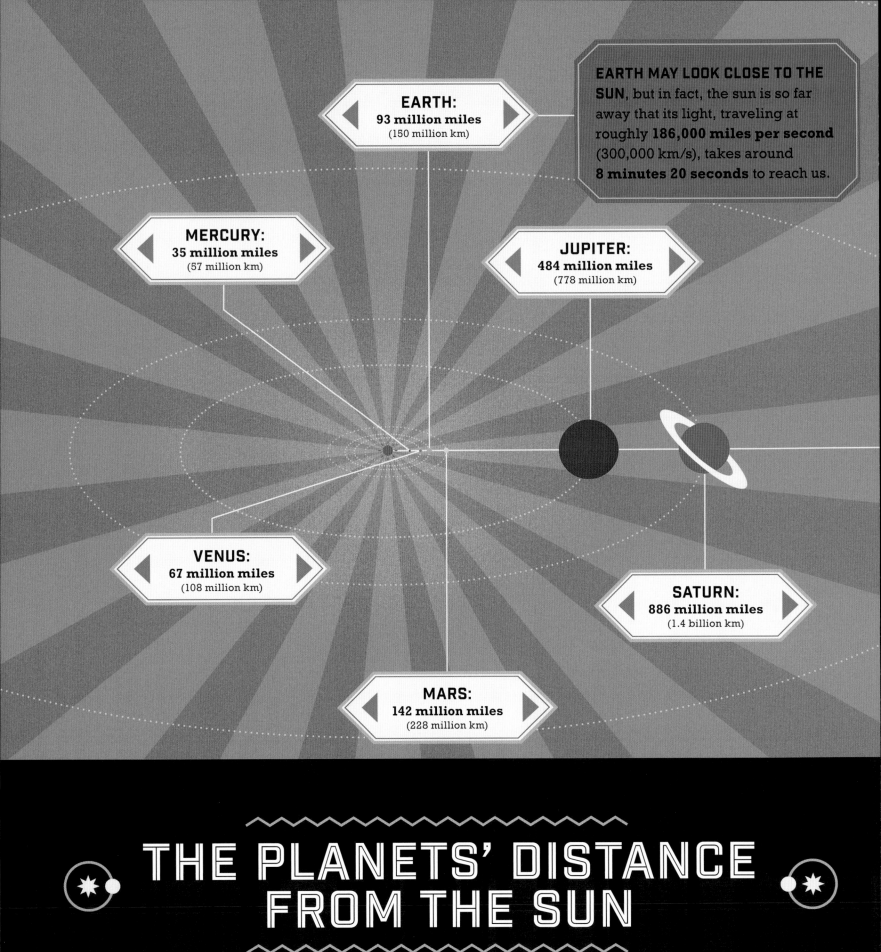

EARTH:
93 million miles
(150 million km)

EARTH MAY LOOK CLOSE TO THE SUN, but in fact, the sun is so far away that its light, traveling at roughly **186,000 miles per second** (300,000 km/s), takes around **8 minutes 20 seconds** to reach us.

MERCURY:
35 million miles
(57 million km)

JUPITER:
484 million miles
(778 million km)

VENUS:
67 million miles
(108 million km)

SATURN:
886 million miles
(1.4 billion km)

MARS:
142 million miles
(228 million km)

THE PLANETS' DISTANCE FROM THE SUN

PLUTO:
3.7 billion miles
(5.9 billion km)

PLUTO IS A DWARF PLANET that's even farther from the sun than Neptune. If you could fly a plane from Earth to Pluto, the trip would take more than **800 years**!

URANUS:
1.8 billion miles
(2.9 billion km)

MOST PLANETS TRAVEL in an elliptical, or oval-shaped, orbit around the sun. This means that the distance from each planet to the sun changes depending where each planet is in its orbit. This graphic shows the average distances between each planet and the sun.

NEPTUNE:
2.8 billion miles
(4.5 billion km)

Space is huge—so big that our solar system alone stretches for billions of miles. At the center of the solar system is the sun. Mercury is the closest planet to the sun. Daytime temperatures on Mercury reach a scorching 801°F (427°C). Neptune is the most distant planet. Large storms whirl through its atmosphere, with winds at speeds of 1,342 mph (2,160 kph), and temperatures are a freezing -353°F (-214°C). Our planet is positioned at just the right distance for sustaining life—it's not too hot and not too cold.

The planets in our solar system vary wildly in size. Below are the diameters of each planet from the smallest to the largest. Check out each planet's size compared to Earth!

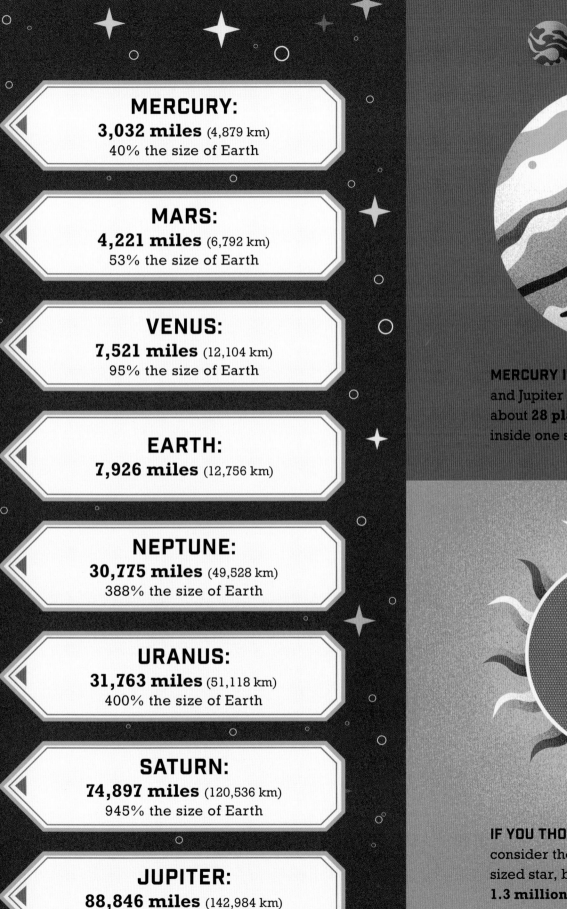

MERCURY:
3,032 miles (4,879 km)
40% the size of Earth

MARS:
4,221 miles (6,792 km)
53% the size of Earth

VENUS:
7,521 miles (12,104 km)
95% the size of Earth

EARTH:
7,926 miles (12,756 km)

NEPTUNE:
30,775 miles (49,528 km)
388% the size of Earth

URANUS:
31,763 miles (51,118 km)
400% the size of Earth

SATURN:
74,897 miles (120,536 km)
945% the size of Earth

JUPITER:
88,846 miles (142,984 km)
1,121% the size of Earth

× 28 =

MERCURY IS THE SMALLEST PLANET and Jupiter is the largest. You could fit about **28 planets** the size of Mercury inside one single Jupiter.

IF YOU THOUGHT JUPITER WAS BIG, consider the sun. It's just an average-sized star, but around **1,000 Jupiters** or **1.3 million Earths** could fit inside it!

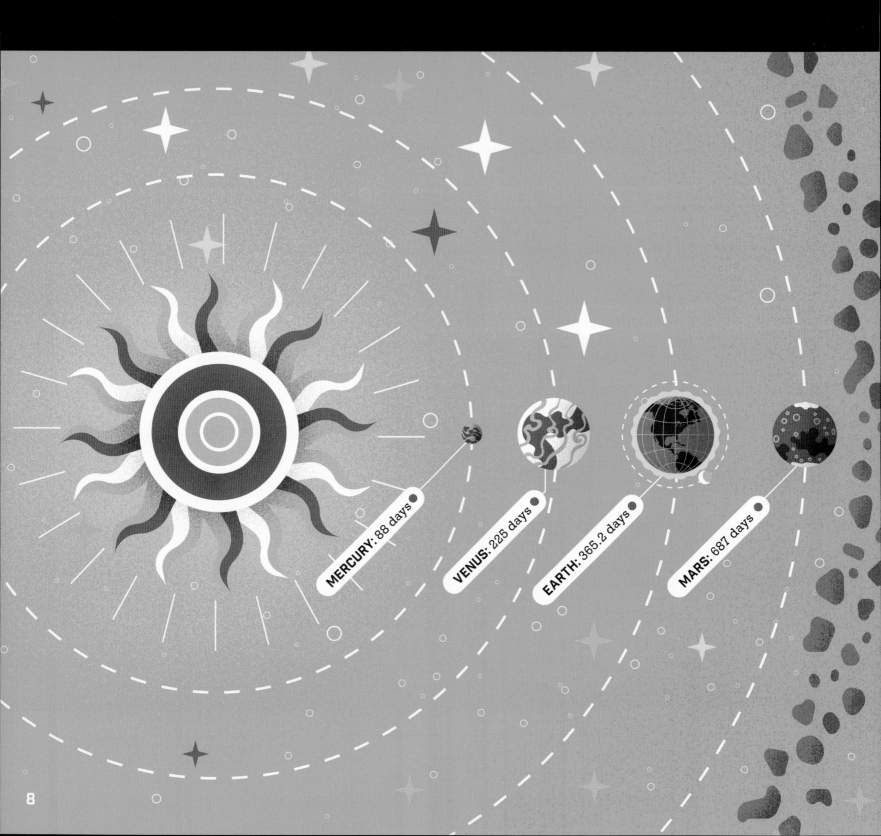

MERCURY: 88 days

VENUS: 225 days

EARTH: 365.2 days

MARS: 687 days

Our solar system is made up of the sun, planets, dwarf planets, comets, moons, meteoroids, and asteroids. All of the planets in our solar system revolve around the sun, but some take much longer than others!

Let's take a look at how many days each planet takes to orbit the sun.

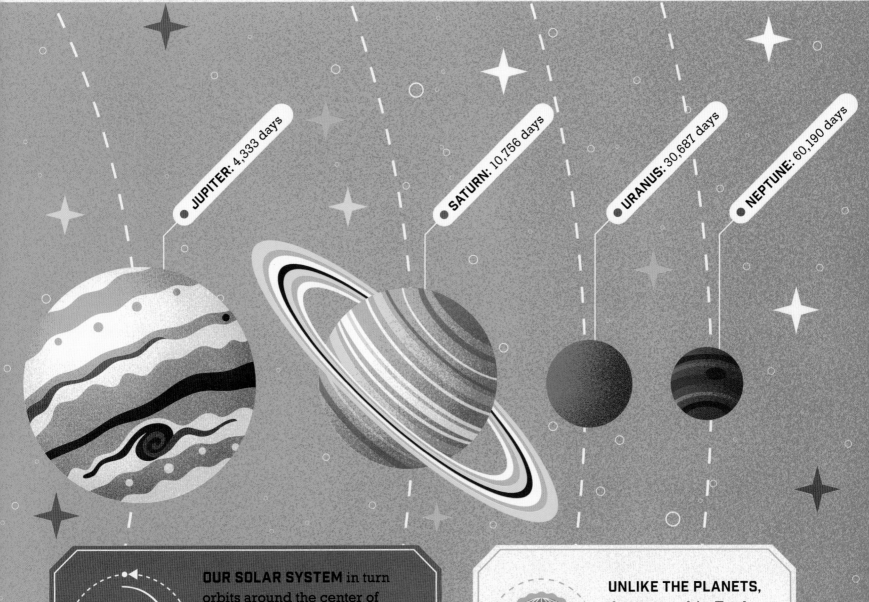

JUPITER: 4,333 days

SATURN: 10,756 days

URANUS: 30,687 days

NEPTUNE: 60,190 days

OUR SOLAR SYSTEM in turn orbits around the center of our galaxy—the Milky Way. Traveling at an average speed of 515,000 mph (828,000 kph), one orbit takes about **230 million years** to complete.

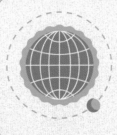

UNLIKE THE PLANETS, the moon orbits Earth instead of the sun. It takes the moon around **27 days** to complete one trip around Earth.

RECORD-BREAKING WEATHER

Hottest
PLACE ON EARTH

134°F
(56.7°C)

Coldest
PLACE ON EARTH

-128.5°F
(-89.2°C)

DEATH VALLEY, USA

VOSTOK STATION, ANTARCTICA

THE HOTTEST AIR TEMPERATURE EVER recorded on Earth was in Death Valley in the Mojave Desert. Despite its sizzling climate, it is home to lizards, snakes, bighorn sheep, desert tortoises, and mountain lions.

THE COLDEST AIR TEMPERATURE EVER recorded was at this Russian research station in East Antarctica. During the long, dark winters, it can get so cold here that humans are unable to breathe the air for longer than a few seconds!

Wettest
PLACE ON EARTH

467 in.
(11,871 mm)

Driest
PLACE ON EARTH

0 in.
(0 mm)

MAWSYNRAM, INDIA

DRY VALLEYS, ANTARCTICA

WITH AN AVERAGE RAINFALL of 467 inches (11,871 mm) per year, residents of this hillside village in northeastern India know to always carry an umbrella!

NOT ONLY IS ANTARCTICA THE COLDEST place on Earth, it is also the driest. No rain has fallen in the continent's Dry Valleys for nearly 2 million years. The environment here is very similar to the surface of Mars.

WILD WATER

71%

of Earth's surface is covered by water.

Of all the water on Earth, about

97%

is saltwater.

The rest is freshwater, much of which makes up glaciers and ice sheets.

If all the ice on Earth melted,
the sea level would rise **230 FEET** (70 m)!

THE EARTH'S SALTWATER IS USUALLY DIVIDED UP INTO FIVE MAIN OCEANS.
The graphic on the right shows how much water they contain, from smallest to biggest. Of course, there are no real boundaries between the five and together they form one giant ocean.

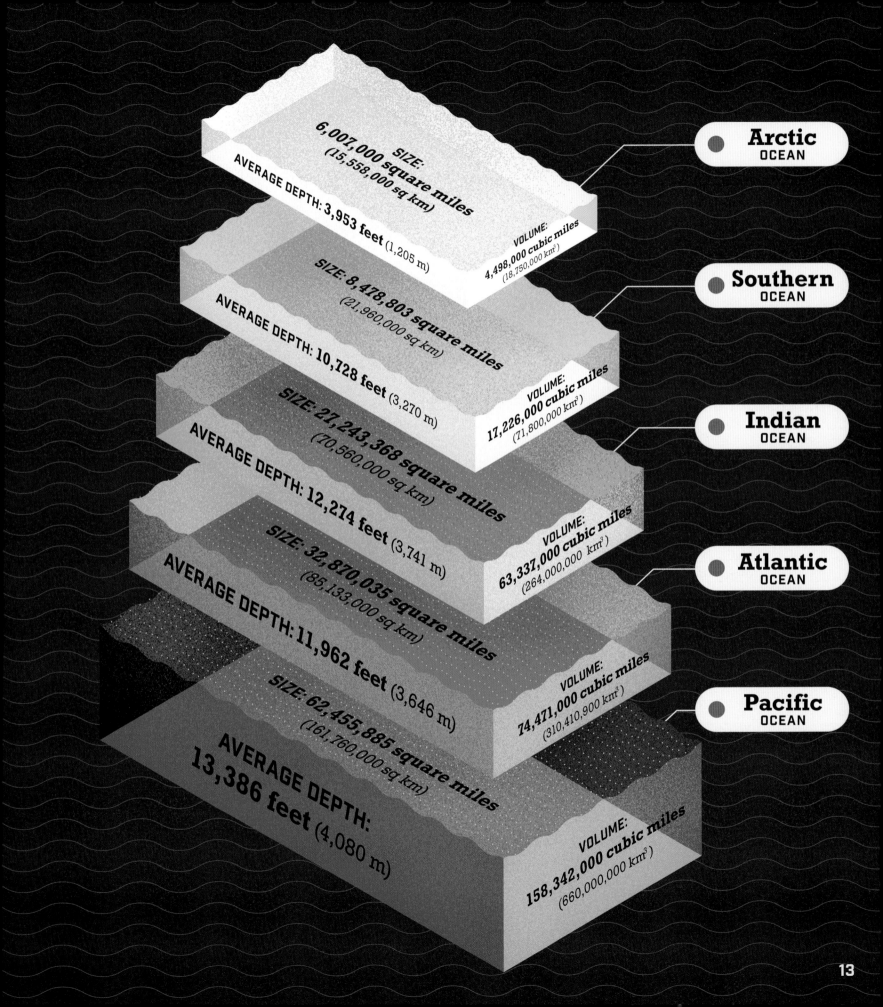

Arctic OCEAN

SIZE: 6,007,000 square miles (15,558,000 sq km)
AVERAGE DEPTH: 3,953 feet (1,205 m)
VOLUME: 4,498,000 cubic miles (18,750,000 km³)

Southern OCEAN

SIZE: 8,478,803 square miles (21,960,000 sq km)
AVERAGE DEPTH: 10,728 feet (3,270 m)
VOLUME: 17,226,000 cubic miles (71,800,000 km³)

Indian OCEAN

SIZE: 27,243,368 square miles (70,560,000 sq km)
AVERAGE DEPTH: 12,274 feet (3,741 m)
VOLUME: 63,337,000 cubic miles (264,000,000 km³)

Atlantic OCEAN

SIZE: 32,870,035 square miles (85,133,000 sq km)
AVERAGE DEPTH: 11,962 feet (3,646 m)
VOLUME: 74,471,000 cubic miles (310,410,900 km³)

Pacific OCEAN

SIZE: 62,455,885 square miles (161,760,000 sq km)
AVERAGE DEPTH: 13,386 feet (4,080 m)
VOLUME: 158,342,000 cubic miles (660,000,000 km³)

AWE-INSPIRING ANIMALS

Meet some of the **largest animals** from around the world!

A **ON EARTH: Blue whale**

Weighing up to a massive **200 tons** (180 tonnes), the blue whale is the biggest animal on our planet. In fact, it's the largest animal to have ever lived. It can grow to **100 feet** (30 m) long, equivalent to two buses, and its tongue alone weighs as much as an elephant!

B **IN EUROPE: European bison**

The European bison can weigh up to **2,200 pounds** (1,000 kg) and grow **6.6 feet** (2 m) tall, making it Europe's largest living land animal. The species was hunted almost to extinction about a hundred years ago, but thanks to conservation efforts, today they can be found grazing in forests and on plains in their thousands.

C **IN NORTH AMERICA: Polar bear**

North America's biggest land predator can weigh as much as **1,700 pounds** (800 kg) and tower more than **10 feet** (3 m) tall on its hind legs.

D **IN SOUTH AMERICA: Tapir**

Tapirs look like pigs, but are related to horses and rhinoceroses. Weighing in at around **660 pounds** (300 kg), they are the continent's heaviest land mammal.

E **IN AFRICA: African elephant**

This gentle giant is not only the biggest land animal in Africa, it is also the largest to walk the Earth. It can weigh as much as **15,000 pounds** (7,000 kg) and stand **12 feet** (3.7 m) tall.

F **IN ASIA: Asian elephant**

Asian elephants are smaller than their African cousins, weighing around **1,300 pounds** (6,000 kg) and reaching **11 feet** (3.4 m) tall.

G **IN ANTARCTICA: Elephant seal**

Named for the trunk-like snout of the adult males, southern elephant seals weigh **8,800 pounds** (4,000 kg). While slow on land, they are amazing swimmers and can stay underwater for up to two hours!

H **IN AUSTRALIA: Red kangaroo**

At **200 pounds** (91 kg) and more than **5.9 feet** (1.8 m) tall, red kangaroos are the largest land mammal in Oceania and the largest marsupial in the world. They use their powerful legs to leap more than **5 feet** (1.5 m) high!

B

C

H

G

D

KANGAROO BABIES
are called joeys
and they're
**smaller than a
cherry** at birth!

F

E

3.3 FT. (1 M)

15

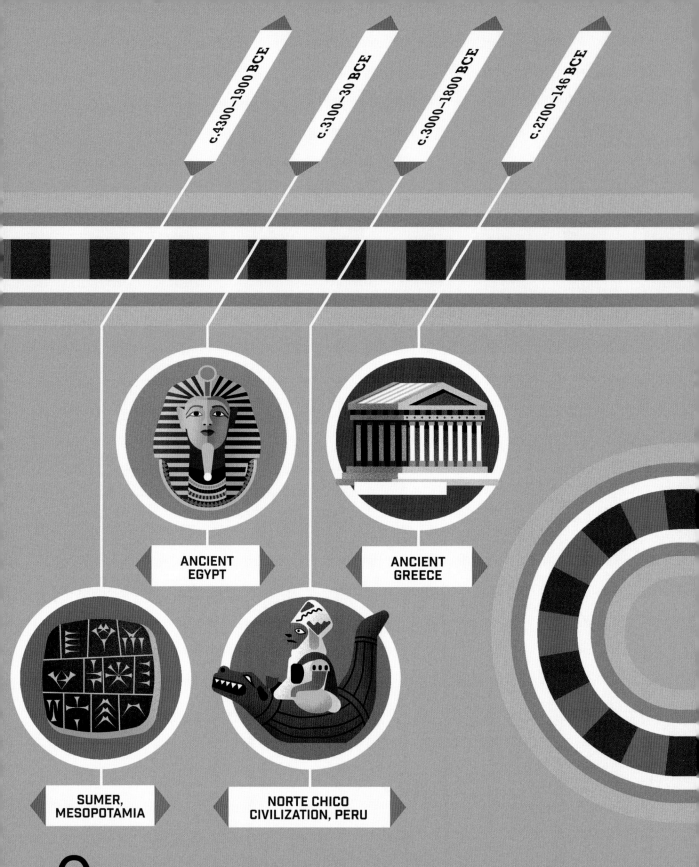

c.4300–1900 BCE

c.3100–30 BCE

c.3000–1800 BCE

c.2700–146 BCE

ANCIENT EGYPT

ANCIENT GREECE

SUMER, MESOPOTAMIA

NORTE CHICO CIVILIZATION, PERU

Around 10,000 BCE, people began to abandon their nomadic, hunter-gatherer lifestyles and live in settled communities. Over time, villages grew into towns and cities, and human societies became more complex, forming civilizations. Here are some of the oldest civilizations, starting with the first.

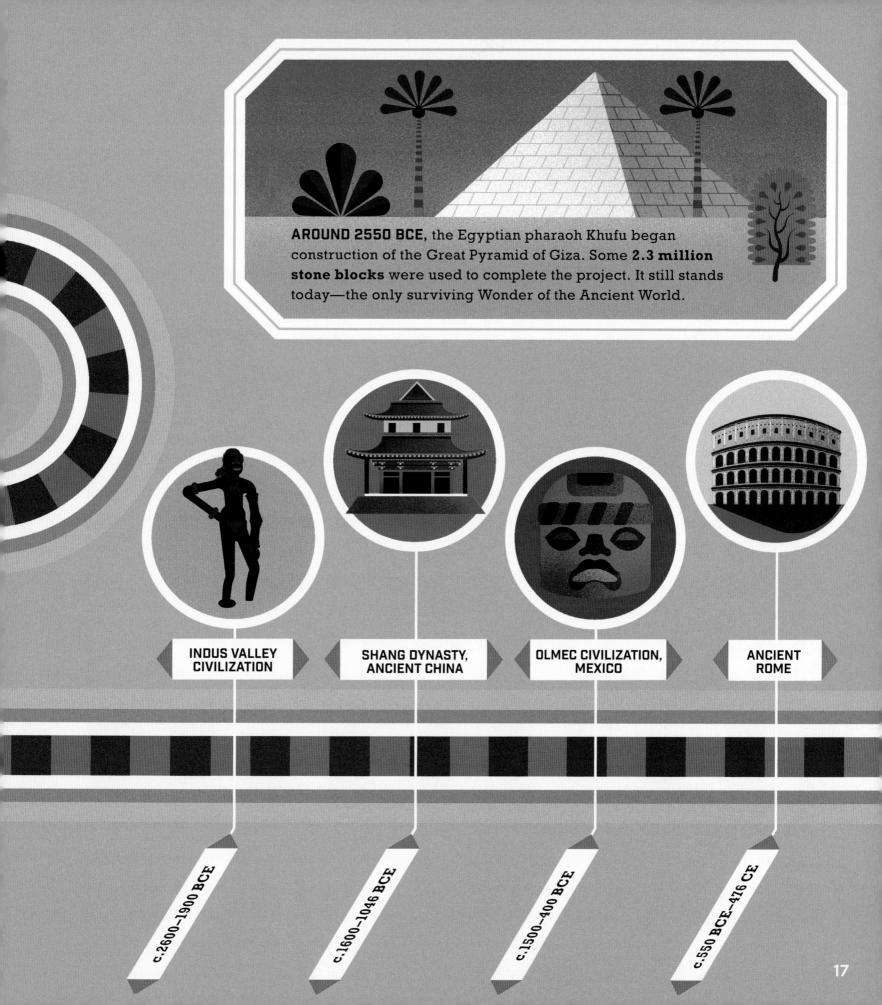

AROUND 2550 BCE, the Egyptian pharaoh Khufu began construction of the Great Pyramid of Giza. Some **2.3 million stone blocks** were used to complete the project. It still stands today—the only surviving Wonder of the Ancient World.

INDUS VALLEY CIVILIZATION

SHANG DYNASTY, ANCIENT CHINA

OLMEC CIVILIZATION, MEXICO

ANCIENT ROME

c.2600–1900 BCE

c.1600–1046 BCE

c.1500–400 BCE

c.550 BCE–476 CE

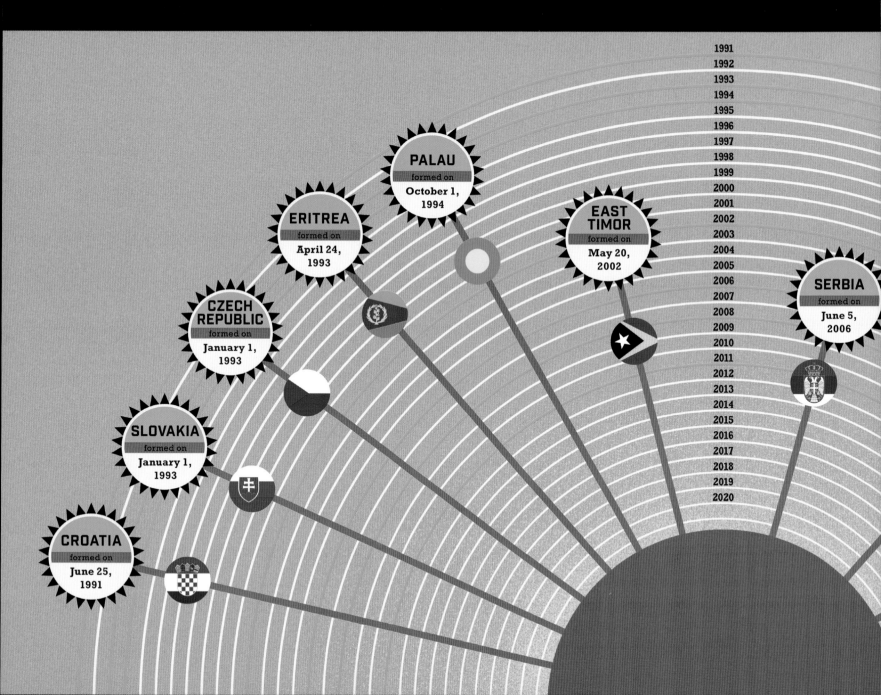

PALAU
formed on
October 1, 1994

ERITREA
formed on
April 24, 1993

EAST TIMOR
formed on
May 20, 2002

SERBIA
formed on
June 5, 2006

CZECH REPUBLIC
formed on
January 1, 1993

SLOVAKIA
formed on
January 1, 1993

CROATIA
formed on
June 25, 1991

1991
1992
1993
1994
1995
1996
1997
1998
1999
2000
2001
2002
2003
2004
2005
2006
2007
2008
2009
2010
2011
2012
2013
2014
2015
2016
2017
2018
2019
2020

There are about 195 countries around the world today. Some are hundreds of years old. Others are still very young, having been founded only recently. Many were established when their people declared independence from another country.

Here are the youngest nations . . .

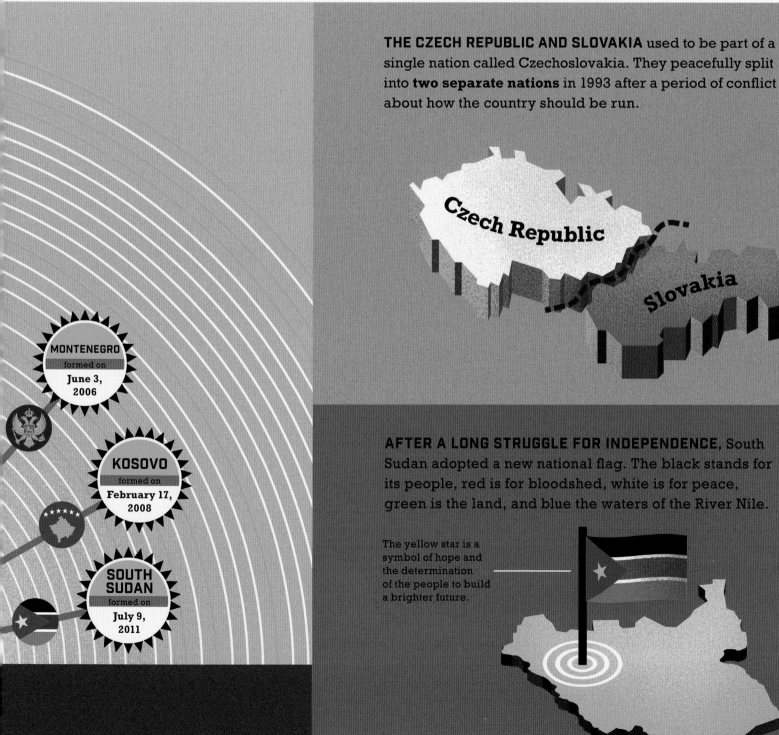

THE CZECH REPUBLIC AND SLOVAKIA used to be part of a single nation called Czechoslovakia. They peacefully split into **two separate nations** in 1993 after a period of conflict about how the country should be run.

Czech Republic

Slovakia

MONTENEGRO
formed on
June 3, 2006

KOSOVO
formed on
February 17, 2008

SOUTH SUDAN
formed on
July 9, 2011

AFTER A LONG STRUGGLE FOR INDEPENDENCE, South Sudan adopted a new national flag. The black stands for its people, red is for bloodshed, white is for peace, green is the land, and blue the waters of the River Nile.

The yellow star is a symbol of hope and the determination of the people to build a brighter future.

From largest to smallest, here is each continent's size and population:

1
ASIA

2
AFRICA

3
NORTH AMERICA

SIZE:	**SIZE:**	**SIZE:**
17,208,000 square miles	**11,608,000 square miles**	**9,449,000 square miles**
(44,569,000 sq km)	(30,065,000 sq km)	(24,473,000 sq km)
POPULATION:	**POPULATION:**	**POPULATION:**
4,641,054,700	**1,340,598,100**	**579,072,200**
59.5% of the world's population	17.2% of the world's population	7.6% of the world's population
48 COUNTRIES	**54 COUNTRIES**	**23 COUNTRIES**

5 COUNTRIES
span more than one continent.

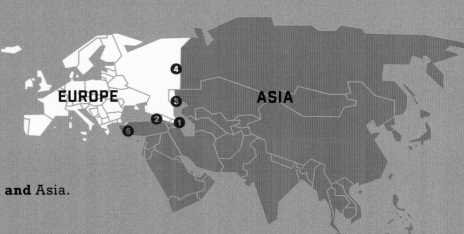

❶ **Azerbaijan,** ❷ **Georgia,** ❸ **Kazakhstan,**
❹ **Russia, and** ❺ **Turkey** are part of Europe **and** Asia.

It is estimated that the world's **total population** is around

7.8 billion

(THAT'S A LOT OF PEOPLE LIVING ON THIS PLANET!)

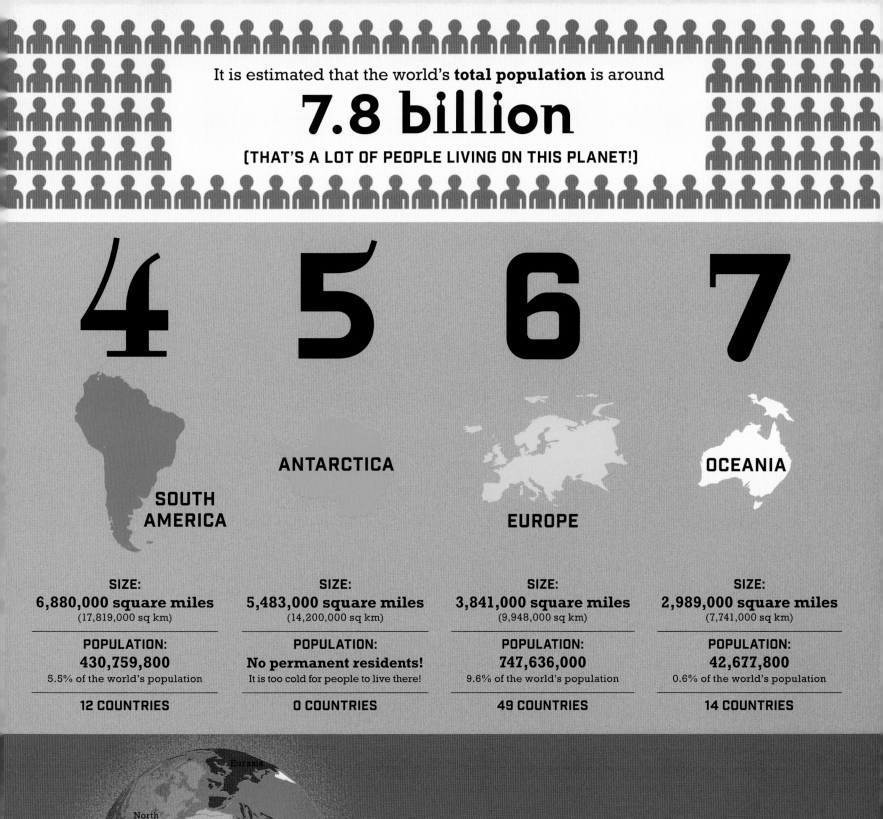

4

SOUTH AMERICA

SIZE:
6,880,000 square miles
(17,819,000 sq km)

POPULATION:
430,759,800
5.5% of the world's population

12 COUNTRIES

5

ANTARCTICA

SIZE:
5,483,000 square miles
(14,200,000 sq km)

POPULATION:
No permanent residents!
It is too cold for people to live there!

0 COUNTRIES

6

EUROPE

SIZE:
3,841,000 square miles
(9,948,000 sq km)

POPULATION:
747,636,000
9.6% of the world's population

49 COUNTRIES

7

OCEANIA

SIZE:
2,989,000 square miles
(7,741,000 sq km)

POPULATION:
42,677,800
0.6% of the world's population

14 COUNTRIES

Eurasia
North America
Africa
South America
India
Antarctica
Australia

AS YOU CAN SEE, the continents look like puzzle pieces that could fit together. That's because they used to be part of the same landmass! It was called Pangea and it started to break apart **175 million years ago.**

Countries come in all shapes and sizes. Some stretch for millions of miles. Others are so little you could easily walk from one end to the other. Incredibly, the top ten biggest countries take up 49 percent of the planet's landmass. The following are the world's largest and smallest.

LARGEST

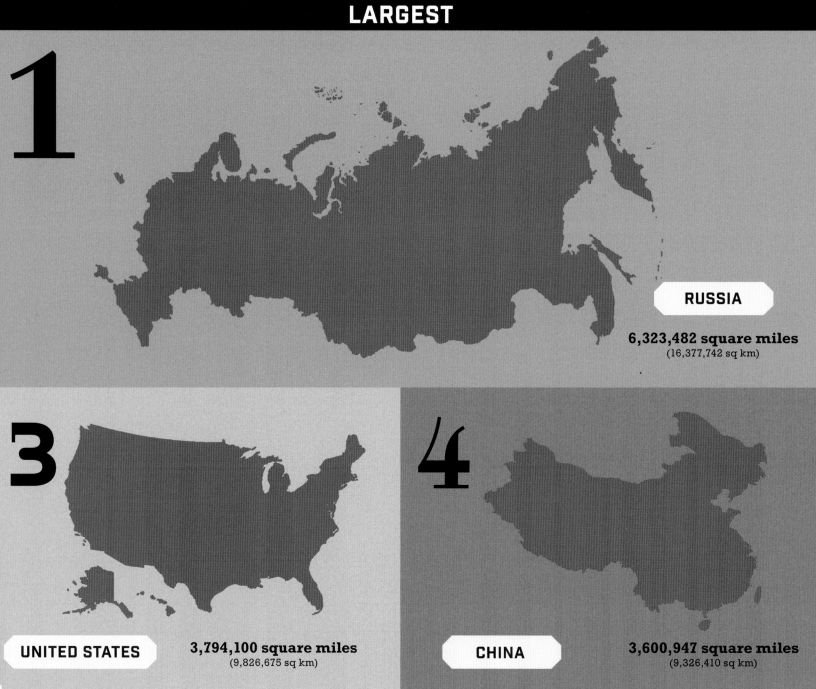

1

RUSSIA

6,323,482 square miles
(16,377,742 sq km)

3

UNITED STATES

3,794,100 square miles
(9,826,675 sq km)

4

CHINA

3,600,947 square miles
(9,326,410 sq km)

VATICAN CITY, SAN MARINO, AND LESOTHO are enclave countries, meaning they are completely surrounded by another country. Italy surrounds Vatican City and San Marino, and South Africa surrounds Lesotho!

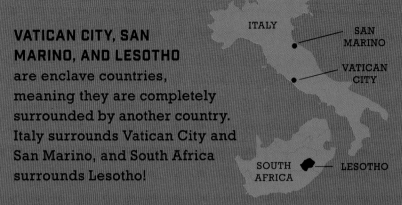

ITALY

SAN MARINO

VATICAN CITY

SOUTH AFRICA — LESOTHO

THE ENTIRE SURFACE AREA OF EARTH, including all the land and all the surface water, totals **197,000,000 square miles** (509,600,000 sq km). Of that, **just 29 percent, or a little under a third, is land.**

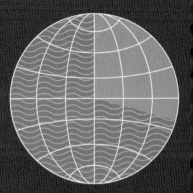

2

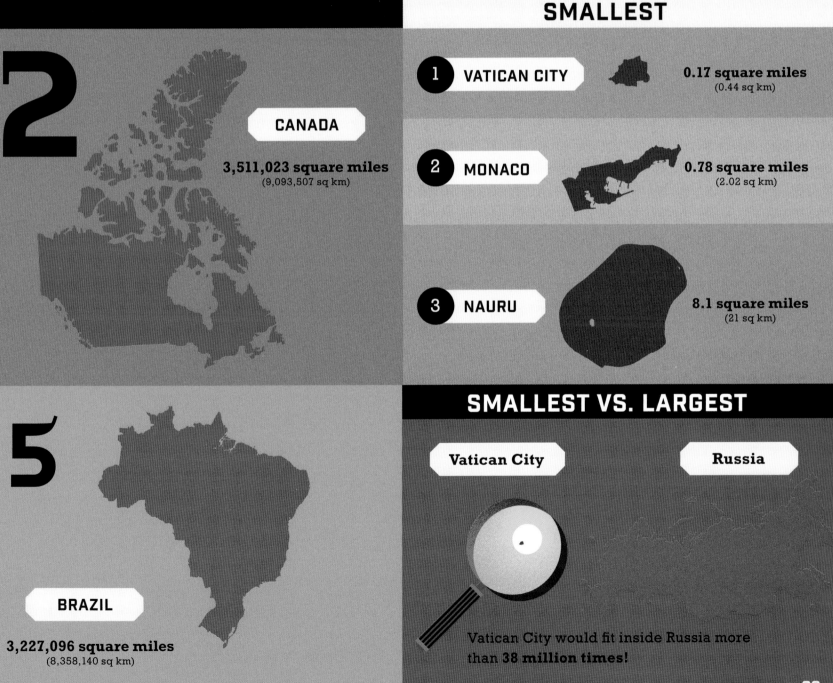

CANADA

3,511,023 square miles
(9,093,507 sq km)

5

BRAZIL

3,227,096 square miles
(8,358,140 sq km)

SMALLEST

1 VATICAN CITY

0.17 square miles
(0.44 sq km)

2 MONACO

0.78 square miles
(2.02 sq km)

3 NAURU

8.1 square miles
(21 sq km)

SMALLEST VS. LARGEST

Vatican City

Russia

Vatican City would fit inside Russia more than **38 million times!**

Some nations are home to many millions of people. Two countries even have billions of people! But others are more sparsely populated—the nation with the smallest population could fit all its residents onto a soccer field! Here are the countries with the most residents compared to those with the fewest!

LARGEST POPULATIONS

= 1,000,000 PEOPLE

CHINA: 1,394,016,000 PEOPLE

INDIA: 1,326,093,000 PEOPLE

SMALLEST POPULATIONS

= 1,000 PEOPLE

VATICAN CITY: 1,000 PEOPLE

NAURU: 11,000 PEOPLE

TUVALU: 11,300 PEOPLE

PALAU: 21,700 PEOPLE

SAN MARINO: 34,200 PEOPLE

LIECHTENSTEIN: 39,000 PEOPLE

LARGEST POPULATIONS

UNITED STATES: 332,639,000 PEOPLE

INDONESIA: 267,026,000 PEOPLE

PAKISTAN: 233,501,000 PEOPLE

NIGERIA: 214,028,000 PEOPLE

BRAZIL: 211,716,000 PEOPLE

BANGLADESH: 162,651,000 PEOPLE

RUSSIA: 141,722,000 PEOPLE

MEXICO: 128,649,000 PEOPLE

SMALLEST POPULATIONS

MONACO: 39,000 PEOPLE

SAINT KITTS & NEVIS: 53,800 PEOPLE

DOMINICA: 74,200 PEOPLE

The population changes constantly. There is

one birth
EVERY 8 SECONDS.

MONACO HAS A SMALL POPULATION but it is the most densely populated country in the world. It has about 39,000 people living in an area that is only 0.78 square miles (2.02 sq km).

I t is estimated that there are just over 7,100 known languages in the world today. Some are spoken by billions of people. Others are so uncommon that fewer than ten people speak them! Here are the top ten languages, starting with the language that is spoken by the most people.

= 100,000,000 (100 million) speakers

❶ ENGLISH ➡ 1.132 BILLION SPEAKERS

Hello!

APPROXIMATELY 16 PERCENT OF THE WORLD'S POPULATION are English speakers and **14 percent** speak Mandarin Chinese.

❷ MANDARIN CHINESE ➡ 1.117 BILLION SPEAKERS

Nǐ hǎo!

ABOUT 290 LANGUAGES ARE SPOKEN IN EUROPE. That may sound like a lot, but **in Asia an estimated 2,300 languages are spoken!**

3 HINDI 637 MILLION SPEAKERS

Namaste!

4 SPANISH 537 MILLION SPEAKERS

¡Hola!

5 FRENCH 280 MILLION SPEAKERS

Bonjour!

6 STANDARD ARABIC 274 MILLION SPEAKERS

Marhaban!

7 BENGALI 265 MILLION SPEAKERS

Nomoskar!

8 RUSSIAN 258 MILLION SPEAKERS

Privet!

9 PORTUGUESE 234 MILLION SPEAKERS

OLÁ!

10 INDONESIAN 199 MILLION SPEAKERS

HALO!

AS MANY AS HALF OF THE WORLD'S LANGUAGES
are expected to be extinct by the end of this century. The Australian Aboriginal
language of Paakyanti is so rare it is thought that **as few as four people** are able to speak it!

Age demographics impact the world's
family dynamics, economy, workforce, and health. In some countries, the number of older people is increasing, as healthcare improves and the mortality rate falls.

Below is a look at age distribution around the world.

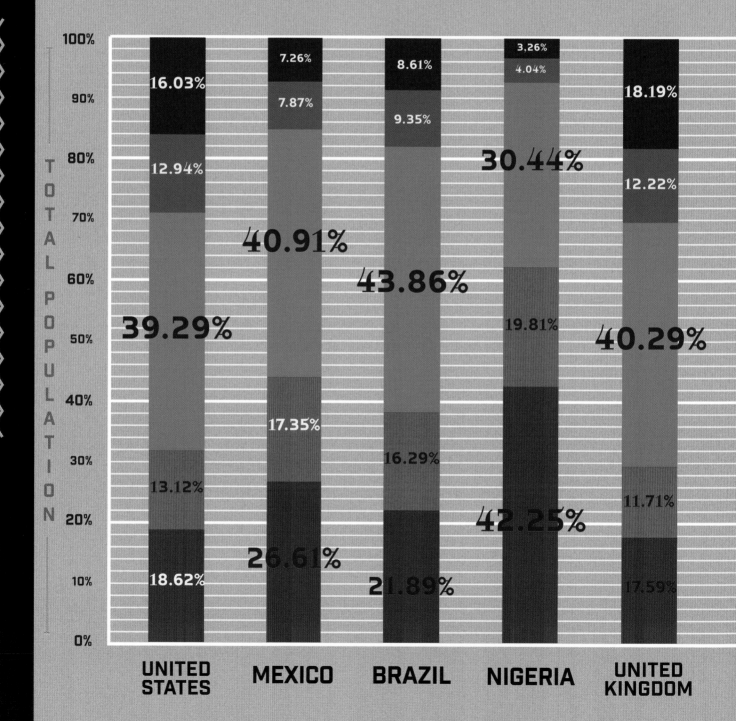

TOTAL POPULATION

	UNITED STATES	MEXICO	BRAZIL	NIGERIA	UNITED KINGDOM
	16.03%	7.26%	8.61%	3.26%	18.19%
	12.94%	7.87%	9.35%	4.04%	12.22%
	39.29%	40.91%	43.86%	30.44%	40.29%
	13.12%	17.35%	16.29%	19.81%	11.71%
	18.62%	26.61%	21.89%	42.25%	17.59%

65+ years
55–64 years
25–54 years
15–24 years
0–14 years

AGE DISTRIBUTION IS IMPACTED BY MANY FACTORS, including

the birth rate, healthcare, wealth, and events such as natural disaster or war.

	RUSSIA	CHINA	INDIA	JAPAN	AUSTRALIA
65+ years	14.66%	11.27%	6.39%	28.38%	15.88%
55–64 years	14.51%	11.35%	7.6%		11.35%
25–54 years	44.21%	47.84%	41.24%	12.01%	41.15%
15–24 years	9.41%	12.32%	17.79%	37.28%	12.89%
0–14 years	17.21%	17.22%	26.98%	9.63%	18.72%
				12.71%	

29

Access to education in one part of the world can be very different from in another. Education can help people's lives in many different ways—improving their minds, increasing the amount of money they can earn, and even raising their levels of health.

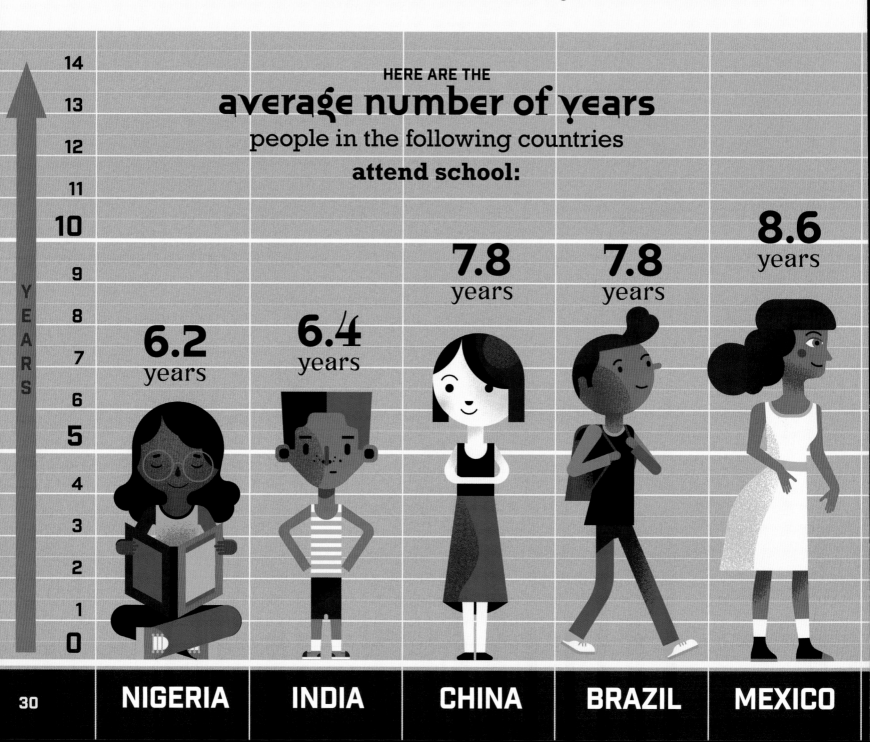

HERE ARE THE
average number of years
people in the following countries
attend school:

YEARS

14
13
12
11
10
9
8
7
6
5
4
3
2
1
0

6.2 years

6.4 years

7.8 years

7.8 years

8.6 years

NIGERIA   **INDIA**   **CHINA**   **BRAZIL**   **MEXICO**

THERE ARE MANY BARRIERS TO EDUCATION across the world, including poverty and lack of funding, schooling space, teachers, and materials. In some places, gender is also a barrier for girls. A recent study showed that about 132 million girls worldwide aged 6–17 do not attend school.

12 years

12.8 years

12.9 years

12.9 years

13.4 years

14

13

12

11

10

9

8

7

5

4

3

2

1

RUSSIA

JAPAN

UNITED KINGDOM

AUSTRALIA

UNITED STATES

Thousands of religions are practiced around the world.

Here are the most common.

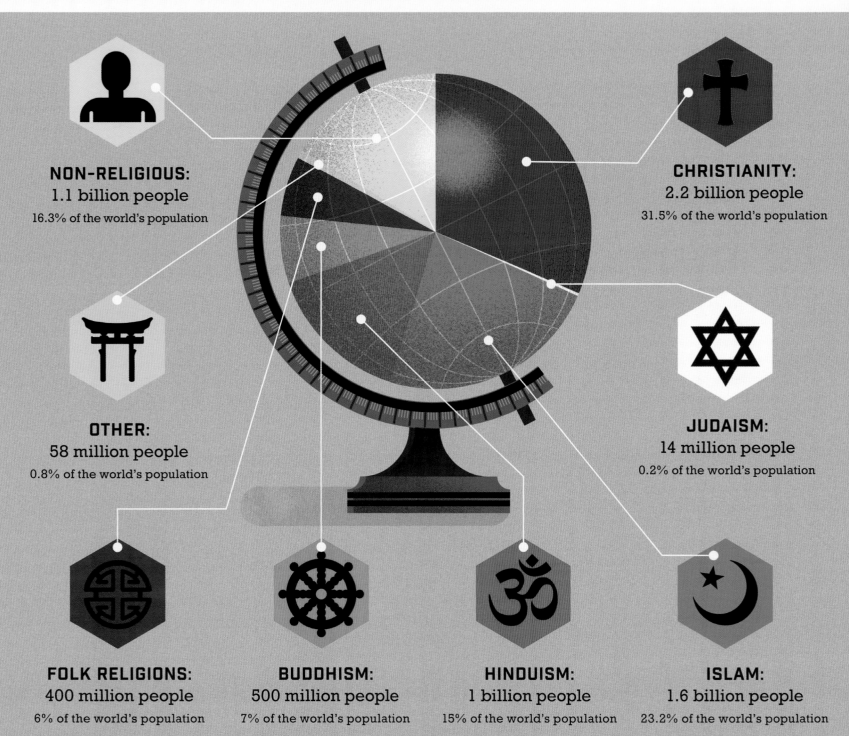

NON-RELIGIOUS:
1.1 billion people
16.3% of the world's population

OTHER:
58 million people
0.8% of the world's population

CHRISTIANITY:
2.2 billion people
31.5% of the world's population

JUDAISM:
14 million people
0.2% of the world's population

FOLK RELIGIONS:
400 million people
6% of the world's population

BUDDHISM:
500 million people
7% of the world's population

HINDUISM:
1 billion people
15% of the world's population

ISLAM:
1.6 billion people
23.2% of the world's population

EVERY COUNTRY'S POPULATION has a different mix of religious beliefs. Compare the religious makeup of these countries across the world.

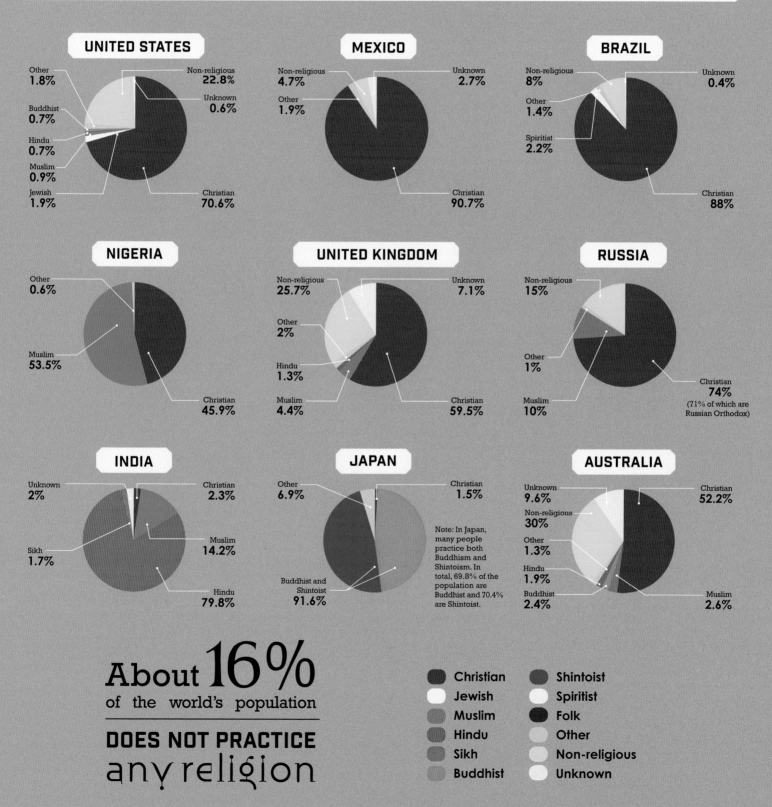

UNITED STATES
- Other 1.8%
- Buddhist 0.7%
- Hindu 0.7%
- Muslim 0.9%
- Jewish 1.9%
- Non-religious 22.8%
- Unknown 0.6%
- Christian 70.6%

MEXICO
- Non-religious 4.7%
- Other 1.9%
- Unknown 2.7%
- Christian 90.7%

BRAZIL
- Non-religious 8%
- Other 1.4%
- Spiritist 2.2%
- Unknown 0.4%
- Christian 88%

NIGERIA
- Other 0.6%
- Muslim 53.5%
- Christian 45.9%

UNITED KINGDOM
- Non-religious 25.7%
- Other 2%
- Hindu 1.3%
- Muslim 4.4%
- Unknown 7.1%
- Christian 59.5%

RUSSIA
- Non-religious 15%
- Other 1%
- Muslim 10%
- Christian 74% (71% of which are Russian Orthodox)

INDIA
- Unknown 2%
- Sikh 1.7%
- Christian 2.3%
- Muslim 14.2%
- Hindu 79.8%

JAPAN
- Other 6.9%
- Christian 1.5%
- Buddhist and Shintoist 91.6%

Note: In Japan, many people practice both Buddhism and Shintoism. In total, 69.8% of the population are Buddhist and 70.4% are Shintoist.

AUSTRALIA
- Unknown 9.6%
- Non-religious 30%
- Other 1.3%
- Hindu 1.9%
- Buddhist 2.4%
- Christian 52.2%
- Muslim 2.6%

About 16%
of the world's population

DOES NOT PRACTICE any religion

Legend:
- Christian
- Jewish
- Muslim
- Hindu
- Sikh
- Buddhist
- Shintoist
- Spiritist
- Folk
- Other
- Non-religious
- Unknown

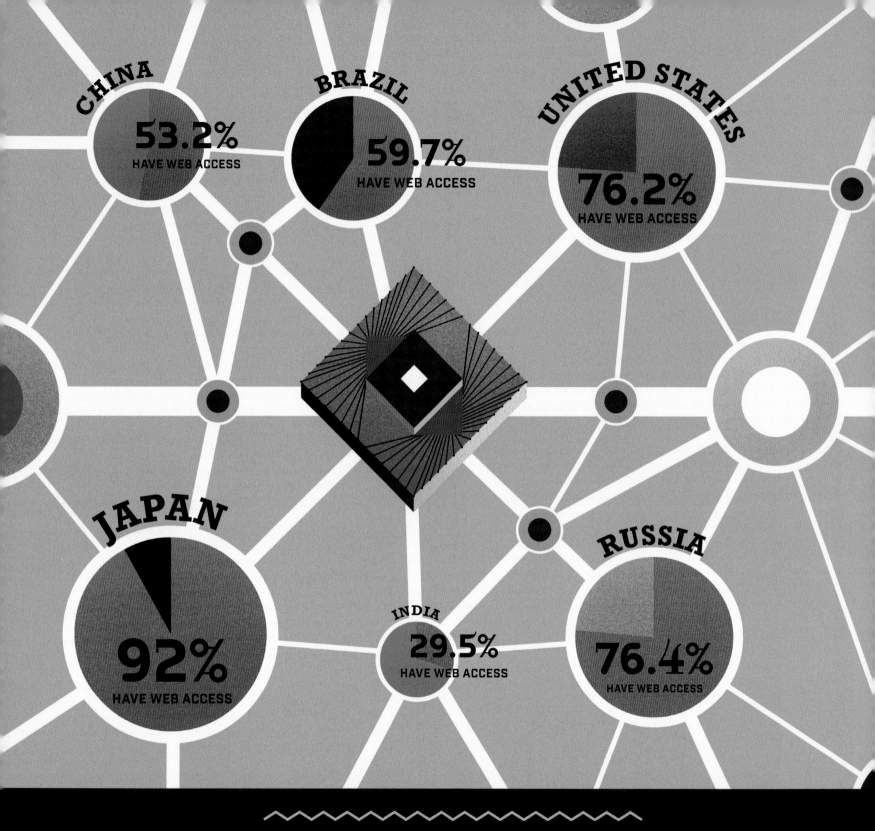

CHINA
53.2%
HAVE WEB ACCESS

BRAZIL
59.7%
HAVE WEB ACCESS

UNITED STATES
76.2%
HAVE WEB ACCESS

JAPAN
92%
HAVE WEB ACCESS

INDIA
29.5%
HAVE WEB ACCESS

RUSSIA
76.4%
HAVE WEB ACCESS

WORLD WIDE WEB

What percentage of a country's people have the ability to use the web?

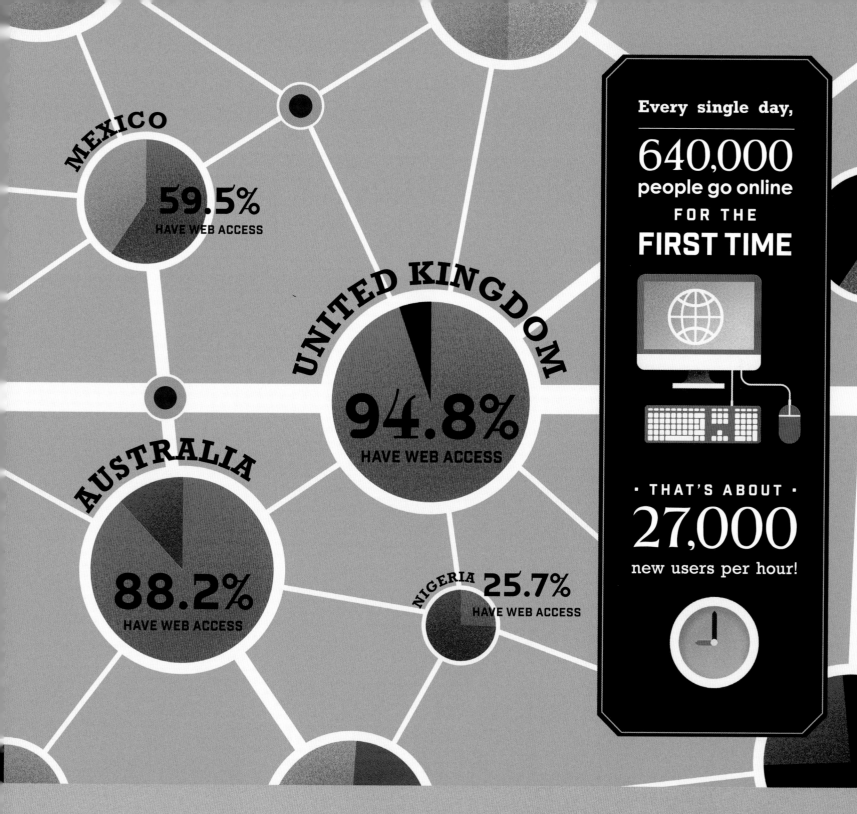

MEXICO
59.5%
HAVE WEB ACCESS

UNITED KINGDOM
94.8%
HAVE WEB ACCESS

AUSTRALIA
88.2%
HAVE WEB ACCESS

NIGERIA **25.7%**
HAVE WEB ACCESS

Every single day,
640,000
people go online
FOR THE
FIRST TIME

· THAT'S ABOUT ·
27,000
new users per hour!

ABOUT **3,174,000,000** PEOPLE
HAVE ACCESS TO THE INTERNET.

That's 43 percent of the world's population that goes online.

CLEAN WATER

Water is essential to life. And yet, about 25 percent of the world's population does not have access to safe drinking water. Here are the ten countries with the lowest access to clean drinking water.

2.1 billion people
around the world
lack safe water at home.

➡ Of those people, **230 MILLION SPEND MORE THAN 30 MINUTES** per round trip collecting water.

ERITREA
19%

PAPUA NEW GUINEA
37%

★ UGANDA
38%

Ethiopia
39%

DEMOCRATIC REPUBLIC of the CONGO
39%

IN MANY COUNTRIES, 100 PERCENT OF THE POPULATION HAVE ACCESS TO IMPROVED DRINKING WATER, or water that is safe from contaminants. Countries with some of the cleanest tap water include Canada, Germany, Norway, Sweden, UK, Switzerland, Singapore, and New Zealand.

RURAL AREAS ARE MORE LIKELY than cities to not have safe drinking water. Of the people worldwide who do not have clean water, 82 percent are in rural areas, while 18 percent are in cities.

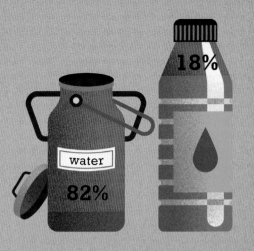

18%

water

82%

ANGOLA

SOMALIA

NIGER

MOZAMBIQUE

41%

40%

43%

CHAD

46%

47%

OUR FURRY FRIENDS

CHINA
53,100,000

USA
74,059,000

RUSSIA
17,800,000

BRAZIL
12,466,000

FRANCE
11,480,000

IN COUNTRIES ALL AROUND THE GLOBE, PEOPLE LOVE THEIR PETS!
About 57 percent of the world's population has an animal friend.

CHINA
27,400,000

USA
69,929,000

RUSSIA
12,520,000

JAPAN
12,000,000

PHILIPPINES
11,600,000

BRAZIL
191,001,000

ITALY
13,000,000

USA
8,300,000

AUSTRALIA
7,800,000

FRANCE
6,200,000

IN THE UNITED STATES
36%
of dog owners
give their canine friends
birthday presents.

Here are the countries with the highest numbers
of pet cats, dogs, birds, and fish.

USA
57,750,000

BRAZIL
26,500,000

AUSTRALIA
20,500,000

FRANCE
37,300,000

UK
20,000,000

THE TALLEST PET DOG ever
measured was a Great Dane
called Zeus. It stood at **3.7 feet**
(111.8 cm)—about the size of a
small pony. The smallest dog
is a Chihuahua called Milly,
who is a mere **3.8 inches**
(9.65 cm) tall—around the
same as a high-heeled shoe.
When she was born, she
could fit on a teaspoon!

39

A bout 54 percent of the world's population live in urban areas, and that number is rising. It is estimated that by 2050, 66 percent of people will live in a metropolitan area. The biggest cities house a staggering number of people. Here are the ten cities with the largest populations.

POPULATION DENSITY

= 5,000 PEOPLE
The figures on the right show the number of people per square mile/kilometer.

TOP 5 ▶
MOST DENSELY POPULATED CITIES IN THE WORLD

POPULATION

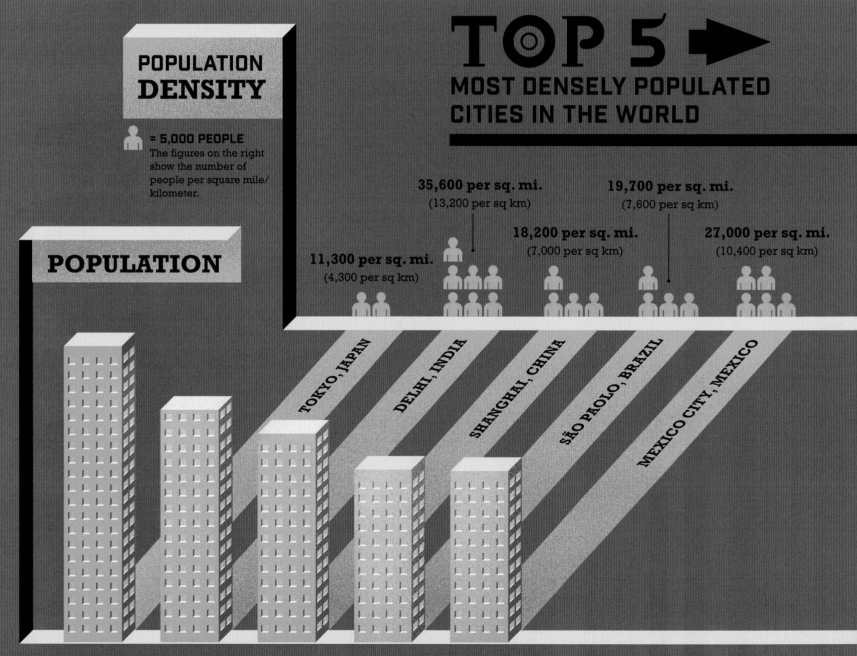

11,300 per sq. mi.
(4,300 per sq km)

35,600 per sq. mi.
(13,200 per sq km)

18,200 per sq. mi.
(7,000 per sq km)

19,700 per sq. mi.
(7,600 per sq km)

27,000 per sq. mi.
(10,400 per sq km)

TOKYO, JAPAN
DELHI, INDIA
SHANGHAI, CHINA
SÃO PAOLO, BRAZIL
MEXICO CITY, MEXICO

37.5 million   28.5 million   25.6 million   21.7 million   21.6 million

SPACE IS SO LIMITED IN TOKYO that hotels with tiny bed-sized rooms have become popular. These capsule hotels feature "pods" stacked in rows for sleeping.

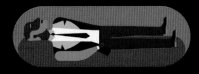
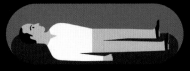
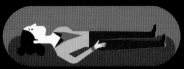

① **Dhaka, Bangladesh**
150.800 people per sq. mi. (58.200 per sq km)

② **Mumbai, India**
94.800 people per sq. mi. (36.600 per sq km)

③ **Surat, India**
73.300 people per sq. mi. (28.300 per sq km)

④ **Hong Kong, China**
69.800 people per sq. mi. (26.900 per sq km)

⑤ **Kinshasa, DR Congo**
58.700 people per sq. mi. (22.600 per sq km)

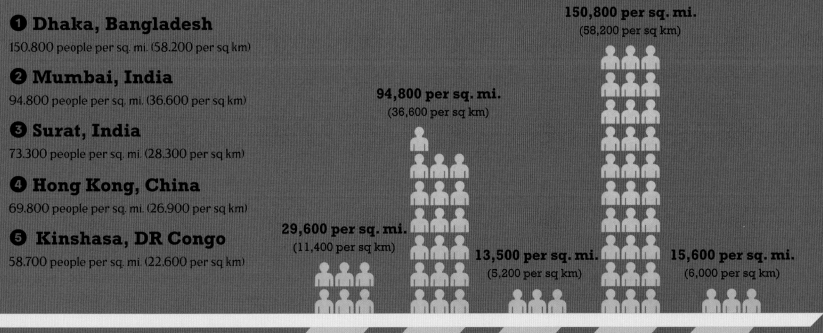

150,800 per sq. mi.
(58,200 per sq km)

94,800 per sq. mi.
(36,600 per sq km)

29,600 per sq. mi.
(11,400 per sq km)

13,500 per sq. mi.
(5,200 per sq km)

15,600 per sq. mi.
(6,000 per sq km)

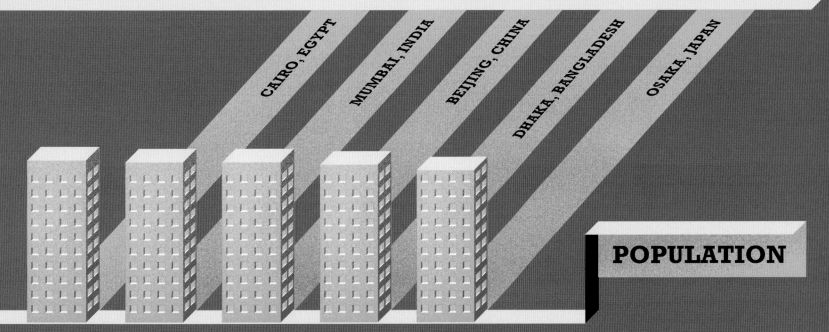

CAIRO, EGYPT

MUMBAI, INDIA

BEIJING, CHINA

DHAKA, BANGLADESH

OSAKA, JAPAN

POPULATION

20.1 million   20 million   19.6 million   19.6 million   19.3 million

Major cities are often well known for their skylines, where tall buildings form a recognizable outline in the sky. The building that currently tops the list for the tallest skyscraper soars so high that it has 163 stories!

SEE HOW THE TOP TEN TALLEST BUILDINGS IN THE WORLD COMPARE TO ONE ANOTHER.

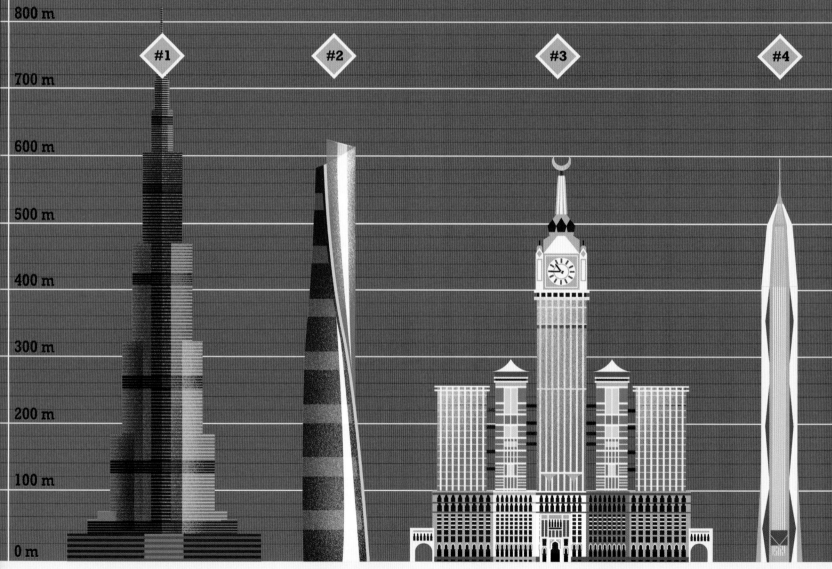

| 800 m |
| 700 m |
| 600 m |
| 500 m |
| 400 m |
| 300 m |
| 200 m |
| 100 m |
| 0 m |

#1   #2   #3   #4

BURJ KHALIFA, Dubai	**SHANGHAI TOWER**	**MAKKAH ROYAL CLOCK TOWER**	**PING AN FINANCE CENTER**
United Arab Emirates	**Shanghai, China**	**Mecca, Saudi Arabia**	**Shenzhen, China**
2,717 feet (828 m)	2,073 feet (632 m)	1,972 feet (601 m)	1,965 feet (599 m)

THE WORLD'S TALLEST BUILDING, the Burj Khalifa, is an incredible 2,717 feet (828 m) high. That's equivalent to around **140 two-story houses** stacked one on top of another.

Skyscrapers are typically taller than 490 feet (150 m) and have at least 40 floors.

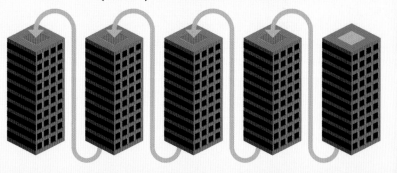

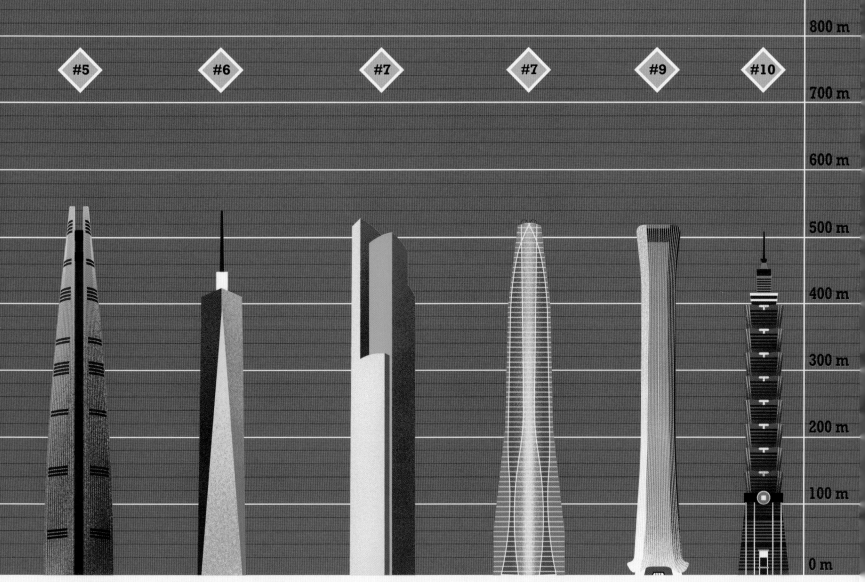

| #5 | #6 | #7 | #7 | #9 | #10 |

| **LOTTE WORLD TOWER** Seoul, South Korea 1,819 feet (554 m) | **ONE WORLD TRADE CENTER** New York City, USA 1,776 feet (541 m) | **CTF FINANCE CENTRE** Guangzhou, China 1,739 feet (530 m) | **CTF FINANCE CENTRE,** Tianjin, China 1,739 feet (530 m) | **CITIC TOWER** Beijing, China 1,731 feet (528 m) | **TAIPEI 101,** Taipei Taiwan, China 1,667 feet (508 m) |

TAKING MASS TRANSIT ISN'T JUST CONVENIENT, it's also better for the environment. Fewer cars on the road means less air pollution and traffic. It's also safer than driving. There are lots of reasons to choose public transportation!

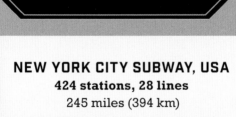

MOSCOW METRO, RUSSIA
236 stations, 15 lines
290 miles (467 km)

NEW YORK CITY SUBWAY, USA
424 stations, 28 lines
245 miles (394 km)
▶ New York's subway has more stations than anywhere else in the world.

BEIJING SUBWAY, CHINA
340 stations, 23 lines
435 miles (699 km)
▶ Beijing has the longest subway system by line length, and with an average of 10.5 million trips per day, it is also one of the world's busiest systems.

MASS TRANSIT AROUND THE WORLD

DELHI METRO, INDIA
229 stations, 12 lines
216 miles (348 km)

GUANGZHOU METRO, CHINA
233 stations, 14 lines
320 miles (515 km)

⑨

LONDON UNDERGROUND, ENGLAND
270 stations, 11 lines
250 miles (402 km)
► In 1863, London became the first city in the world to have underground trains. They were powered by steam, and the tunnels were often filled with smoke!

②

⑥

SHANGHAI METRO, CHINA
345 stations, 17 lines
420 miles (676 km)

MADRID METRO, SPAIN
242 stations, 13 lines
182 miles (293 km)

④

⑦

SEOUL METROPOLITAN SUBWAY, SOUTH KOREA
331 stations, 23 lines
220 miles (353 km)

NOTE: New stations and lines are opening all the time, so these figures are constantly changing. Lengths are total route lengths, not track lengths.

Major cities need to be able to transport a very large number of people each day. To accommodate all these commuters, every metropolitan area has a system of public transportation. Whether it's a train, bus, or ferry, these help large numbers of people to get around.

Here are the ten biggest metro (underground railway) systems in the world by the number of stations—as well as some of the longest, busiest, and oldest.

H ere are the top ten most visited cities in the world, in order from most to least visitors per year:

BANGKOK, THAILAND
22.8 million

PARIS, FRANCE
19.1 million

LONDON, ENGLAND
19 million

DUBAI, UNITED ARAB EMIRATES
15.9 million

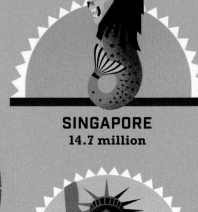

SINGAPORE
14.7 million

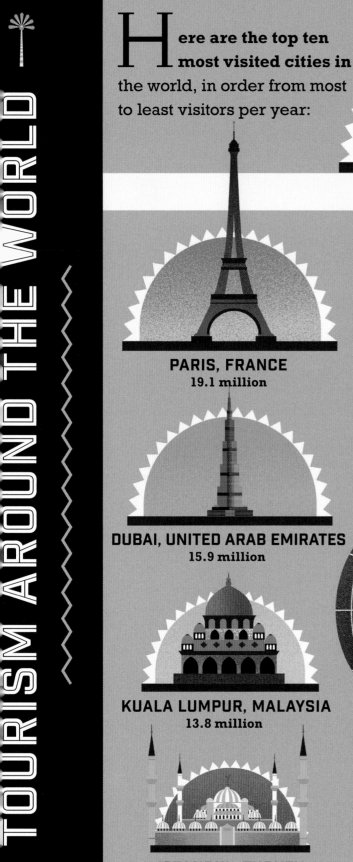

KUALA LUMPUR, MALAYSIA
13.8 million

NEW YORK, USA
13.6 million

ISTANBUL, TURKEY
13.4 million

TOKYO, JAPAN
12.9 million

ANTAYLA, TURKEY
12.4 million

These are the top ten most visited monuments around the world. Have you visited any? If so, you were in good company. These tourist hot spots get millions of visitors every year.

This list includes palaces, historical monuments, and historic sites, but not churches, religious shrines, or pilgrimage sites.

Forbidden City
BEIJING, CHINA
17 million

Palace of Versailles
FRANCE
8.1 million

RELIGIOUS SITES are also popular attractions. The Meiji Jingu Shrine, located in a forest right next to the bustling crowds of Tokyo, has millions of visitors each year. Entry to the shrine is free and a nice break from the activity of the big city.

Lincoln Memorial, Washington, D.C.
USA
7.8 million

CITY PARKS, MARKETS, AND SQUARES are other tourist hot spots. Every year, around 40 million people flock to the bright lights of Times Square in New York City, USA.

Colosseum, Rome
ITALY
7.7 million

Taj Mahal, Agra
INDIA
7.5 million

Parthenon, Athens
GREECE
7.2 million

Eiffel Tower, Paris
FRANCE
6.2 million

Peterhof Palace, St. Petersburg,
RUSSIA
5.2 million

Vietnam Veterans Memorial, Washington, D.C.
USA
4.7 million

MMMM

SLURP

PIZZA